20TH CENTURY DESIGN

70s & 80s

THE HIGH-TECH AGE

For a free color catalog describing Gareth Stevens Publishing's list of high-quality books and multimedia programs, call 1-800-542-2595 (USA) or 1-800-461-9120 (Canada). Gareth Stevens Publishing's Fax: (414) 332-3567.

Library of Congress Cataloging-in-Publication Data available upon request from publisher.
Fax: (414) 332-3567 for the attention of the Publishing Records Department.

ISBN 0-8368-2709-0

This North American edition first published in 2000 by
Gareth Stevens Publishing
A World Almanac Education Group Company
330 West Olive Street, Suite 100
Milwaukee, Wisconsin 53212 USA

Original edition © 1999 by David West Children's Books. First published in Great Britain in 1999 by Heinemann Library, Halley Court, Jordan Hill, Oxford OX2 8EJ, a division of Reed Educational and Professional Publishing Limited. This U.S. edition © 2000 by Gareth Stevens, Inc. Additional end matter © 2000 by Gareth Stevens, Inc.

Picture Research: Brooks Krikler Research

Gareth Stevens Senior Editor: Dorothy L. Gibbs
Gareth Stevens Series Editor: Christy Steele

Photo Credits:
Abbreviations: (t) top, (m) middle, (b) bottom, (l) left, (r) right

Airbus: pages 26(both), 26-27.
Alitalia: page 9(m).
Apple Macintosh: pages 20-21(b).
Braun: page 23(m).
Corbis: Cover (tl, m, br), pages 4-5, 5(ml), 12-13, 13(br), 15(b), 16, 17(bl), 18(l), 18-19, 19, 20.
Dyson: page 11(l).
Eye Ubiquitous: page 8(l).
GEC Computers Ltd.: pages 20-21(t).
JVC: page 22(t).
Kobal Collection: page 17(br).
Norman McGrath: pages 16-17.
NASA: pages 3, 4, 28(all), 29(all).
Paul Nightingale: pages 14-15.
Clare Oliver: page 17(tr).
Olivetti: page 23(t).
Redferns: page 15(t) / G. Chin: page 6(bl) / E. Echenberg: page 5(br) / J. Krsteske: page 7(br).
Science & Society: pages 22-23.
Solution Pictures: Cover (tr, bl), pages 5(mr), 21, 25(tr), 27(t).
Frank Spooner Pictures: Cover (bm), pages 6-7, 9(t), 11(r), 18(r), 24(both), 24-25, 25(m), 27(bl, br).
© Vogue/Condé Nast Publications Ltd.: Willie Christie: page 7(bl) / Patrick Demarchelier:
Cover (ml), page 6(br) / Arthur Elgort: pages 6(tl), 8(br) / Lothar Schmid: page 7(m).
Courtesy of Wolfgang Weingart: page 14(t).

Printed in Mexico

1 2 3 4 5 6 7 8 9 04 03 02 01 00

20TH CENTURY DESIGN

70s & 80s
THE HIGH-TECH AGE

Jackie Gaff and John Tyrrell

Gareth Stevens Publishing
A WORLD ALMANAC EDUCATION GROUP COMPANY

CONTENTS

When it opened in 1977, the high-tech Pompidou Center in Paris turned architecture inside out. It was designed by Italy's Renzo Piano and Britain's Richard Rogers.

In 1981, the American space agency, NASA, launched the first-ever reusable spacecraft, the Space Shuttle Columbia.

TURBULENT TIMES

The 1970s and 1980s were decades of rapid and, sometimes, violent changes. Wars in the Middle East, Vietnam, Afghanistan, and the Falklands; the Watergate scandal in the United States; assassinations of government leaders in India and Egypt; and IRA and PLO terrorist campaigns all contributed to a general climate of political unrest. Unstable economies moved back and forth between boom and bust. Battling an oil crisis in the early 1970s, nations sank into recession, then recovered to enjoy renewed prosperity in the 1980s. That decade, however, ended with financial insecurity when the stock market collapsed on October 19, 1987 — Black Monday. Meanwhile, an electronic revolution was heating up, with microprocessors transforming everything from washing machines to the space program. Design and architecture were changing, too. Postmodernist wit and punk anarchy turned the severe formality of modernism upside down.

"I love New York" is one of the most enduring symbols of the 1970s.

Computer-controlled robots revolutionized industry in the 1970s and 1980s.

Micro-processors first went on sale in 1971.

This "singing" kettle, designed by Michael Graves, is a famous example of postmodern playfulness.

Punk style was meant to be shocking. It was an expression of the frustration over high unemployment in the 1970s.

5

FASHION FREEDOM

The 1970s and 1980s saw extremes in fashion as much as in other fields of design. With people pushing free expression to the limits, styles changed almost daily.

GOING TO EXTREMES

Antiwar protesters of the 1970s mocked the military by donning army surplus clothing. Leather, flannel, and denim were popular, too, with both men and women flaunting macho styles and work wear. As a refuge from rising unemployment and social inequality, some fashions were simply an escape into fantasy, glamour, or nostalgia for the past. Rock stars started some of the most outrageous trends — hair got longer, platform boots got higher, and trousers flared wider.

Retro designs at the end of the 1980s revived the flares of the 60s and 70s.

John Travolta discoed his way to fame in Saturday Night Fever. (1978)

BOYS WILL BE GIRLS WILL BE BOYS

Unisex garments, such as jeans and T-shirts, of the 1960s and 1970s led to a fashion for androgyny (looking both masculine and feminine) in the late 1980s. Girls dressed as boys, and boys dressed as girls.

Pop singer Boy George was the most famous gender bender of the 1980s.

This jacket by Rei Kawakubo is from 1988, the year she declared "red is the new black."

6

THE STRETCH OF TEXTILE TECHNOLOGY

Lycra is the trademark of a synthetic elastic fiber introduced by the Du Pont company in 1958. To maximize its stretch and strength and improve its feel and drape, Lycra is always mixed with another fiber (shown in purple). Lycra can be: (**1**) covered with another fiber, (**2**) twisted with another fiber as it is spun, or (**3**) forced through an air jet to coat the Lycra with lacelike strands of another fiber.

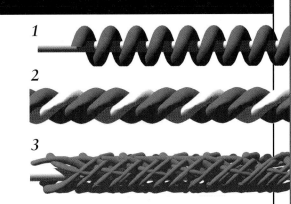

DISCO TO PUNK

Discomania and a growing passion for exercise in the 1970s brought synthetic fabrics, such as stretchy Lycra, into their own. Punks, on the other hand, led an antifashion brigade in their ripped clothes with safety-pin jewelry.

Punk met haute couture in Zandra Rhodes's Punk Chic collection of 1977 — the safety pins are gold!

WEST MEETS EAST

By the early 1980s, the frilly shirts of the new romantics heralded a shift toward nostalgic retro styles. In contrast, yuppie businesswomen were wearing masculine power suits. At the same time, however, Japanese designers, such as Issey Miyake (*b.*1935), Rei Kawakubo (*b.*1942), and Yohji Yamamoto (*b.*1943), were revolutionizing tailored clothing, draping and layering fabrics to create sculptural works of art.

Feathered hats and lace shirts turned the new romantics of the early 1980s into swashbuckling pirates.

More than a few eyebrows were raised as punks "styled" their hair with razors, glue, and brightly colored dyes.

SPORTS TECHNOLOGY

Keeping fit became a worldwide obsession during the 1970s and 1980s. Thousands of people took up aerobics, weight lifting, jogging, cycling, roller-skating, or even marathon running. The development of new sports and high-tech sportswear and equipment fed the fitness craze.

A mountain bike's light-weight frame is made of aluminum, titanium, or carbon-fiber reinforced plastic.

CLIMB EVERY MOUNTAIN

Like many new sports of the period, mountain biking started in the United States. When motorcycles were banned from dirt trails in California's national parks, riders responded by switching to bicycles. Customizing bikes to cope with the rugged conditions of the trails led to their distinctive design — flat, motorcycle-style handlebars; sturdy frames; strong brakes; fat tires; and, of course, many low gears for taking on steep mountain inclines.

Skateboards were first manufactured in the United States in the 1960s. Skateboarding became an international sport in the 1970s.

Inline skates were invented in the late 1970s so an ice-hockey player would have skates to train with in summer or winter.

In the early 1970s, the growth of hang gliding as a sport prompted the development of engine-powered hang gliders, called ultralights.

FLYING WITH THE BIRDS

The history of hang gliding starts in the 1890s, when German engineer Otto Lilienthal (1848–1896) built and tested a series of gliding machines as part of his pioneering efforts to unlock the secrets of heavier-than-air flight. The modern sport of hang gliding began in California during the 1960s. The introduction of high-tech materials, such as carbon-fiber reinforced plastics, encouraged development of the sport.

Otto Lilienthal made more than 2,000 glider flights before tragically plummeting to his death in 1896.

LIGHTWEIGHT TECHNOLOGY

Sport often means "speed," and reducing weight is an important way to gain a winning edge. Technological breakthroughs in the 1960s included the discovery of strong but lightweight materials, such as carbon-fiber reinforced plastics. These plastics are much lighter than steel but can be up to eight times stronger. By the 1970s and 1980s, lightweight plastics had replaced steel in a wide range of sports equipment, from mountain bikes to hang gliders to racing cars, as well as in the space and aircraft industries.

CARBON FIBER — THE LIGHTWEIGHT HEAVYWEIGHT

Carbon fibers were first made in the 1960s at the Farnborough Aircraft Establishment in Britain. Inside each hairlike fiber, tiny carbon crystals are bonded together in long rows. Because of their crystalline structure, carbon fibers are very strong. Even stronger than individual fibers, however, are carbon-fiber laminates, in which layers of carbon fibers are built up at angles to one another.

In carbon fibers, carbon crystals are aligned.

In carbon-fiber laminates, carbon fibers are at angles to one another.

POSTMODERNISM

The word *postmodernism* means "after modernism." It describes movements in art and architecture reacting against the modernist style that dominated design for much of the 20th century.

LESS IS MORE

Modernists believed that form should follow function. In other words, the appearance of a building or an object should be determined by its use. Modernists rejected historical styles and unnecessary decoration in favor of simple, geometric forms and neutral colors, such as black and white. The phrase "less is more," which summarized modernist theory, was coined by one of the leading modernist architects, German-born American Ludwig Mies van der Rohe (1886–1969). This architect's most famous work is the stark, steel and glass Seagram Building in New York City (1959).

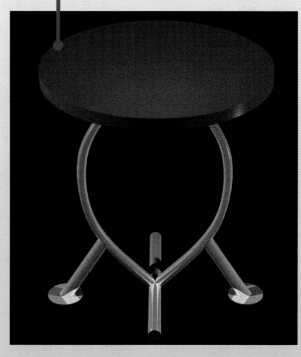

Postmodern Italian architect-designer Michele De Lucchi (b.1951) created this colorful table, exotically named the Cairo table, in 1986.

LESS IS A BORE

In the mid 1960s, the phrase "less is a bore" expressed a growing revolt against the minimalism of the modernists. American architect Robert Venturi (*b.*1925) created this phrase in response to Mies van der Rohe's. For the next two decades, postmodernists like Venturi argued that buildings and objects should be more than simply functional.

The little plastic bird on this kettle's spout whistles when the water boils. American architect and designer Michael Graves (b.1934) created this humorous postmodern icon in 1985 for the Italian manufacturer Alessi.

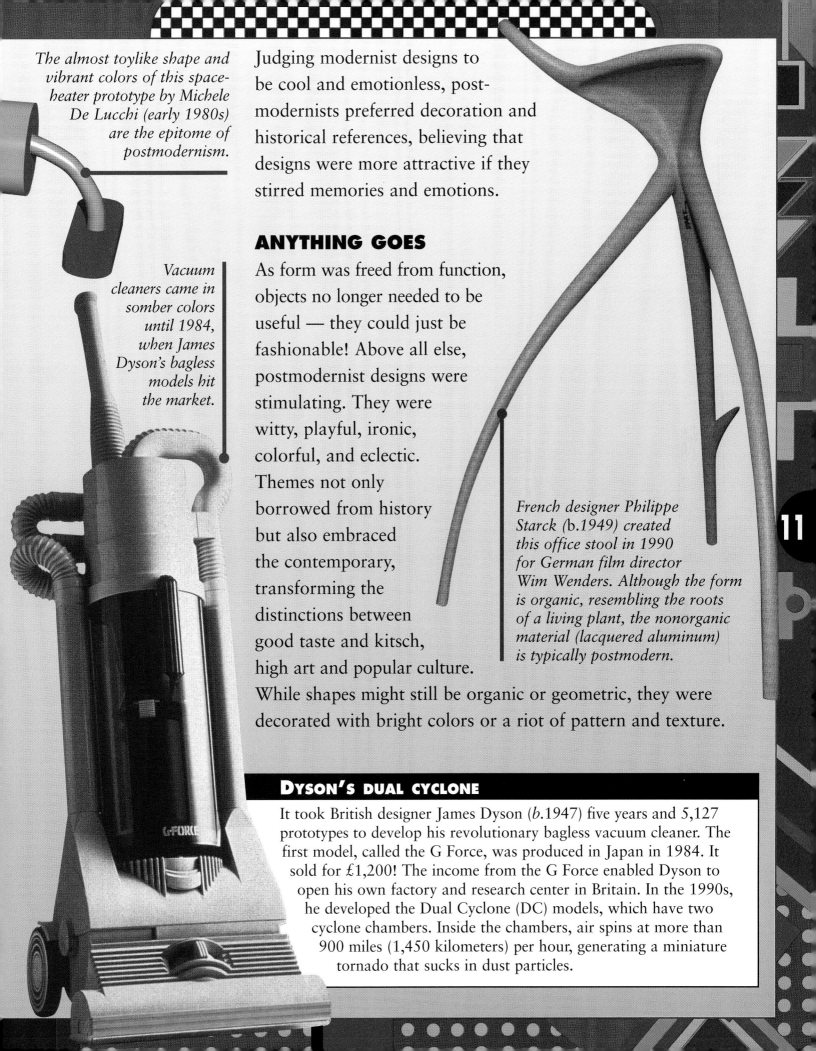

The almost toylike shape and vibrant colors of this space-heater prototype by Michele De Lucchi (early 1980s) are the epitome of postmodernism.

Judging modernist designs to be cool and emotionless, post-modernists preferred decoration and historical references, believing that designs were more attractive if they stirred memories and emotions.

ANYTHING GOES

Vacuum cleaners came in somber colors until 1984, when James Dyson's bagless models hit the market.

As form was freed from function, objects no longer needed to be useful — they could just be fashionable! Above all else, postmodernist designs were stimulating. They were witty, playful, ironic, colorful, and eclectic. Themes not only borrowed from history but also embraced the contemporary, transforming the distinctions between good taste and kitsch, high art and popular culture.

French designer Philippe Starck (b.1949) created this office stool in 1990 for German film director Wim Wenders. Although the form is organic, resembling the roots of a living plant, the nonorganic material (lacquered aluminum) is typically postmodern.

While shapes might still be organic or geometric, they were decorated with bright colors or a riot of pattern and texture.

DYSON'S DUAL CYCLONE

It took British designer James Dyson (b.1947) five years and 5,127 prototypes to develop his revolutionary bagless vacuum cleaner. The first model, called the G Force, was produced in Japan in 1984. It sold for £1,200! The income from the G Force enabled Dyson to open his own factory and research center in Britain. In the 1990s, he developed the Dual Cyclone (DC) models, which have two cyclone chambers. Inside the chambers, air spins at more than 900 miles (1,450 kilometers) per hour, generating a miniature tornado that sucks in dust particles.

FANTASY FURNISHINGS

Postmodern ideas freed designers to radically rethink furniture and interiors. They broke all the rules, adding rich decoration to minimalist forms and combining expensive materials with kitsch colors and patterns.

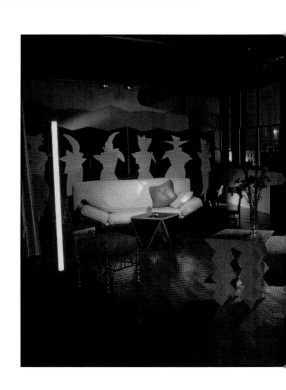

Aztec art and the interiors of 1950s coffee bars inspired Ettore Sottsass to create his lurid Carlton sideboard, made of wood and plastic laminates. Sottsass created this piece for the Memphis group's first exhibition in 1981.

The circles and cones of the Bay table lamp (1983) by Ettore Sottsass echo the geometric forms of modernism, but the brilliantly colored glass adds a definite postmodern touch.

DESIGN DYNAMITE

The Italian design group Memphis burst onto the international postmodernist scene in September 1981. Memphis was the most influential new design movement of the decade; the group had enormous impact worldwide. Its founding father was Italian architect and designer Ettore Sottsass (*b.*1917). Other founding members included Michele De Lucchi from Italy, George Sowden (*b.*1942) from Britain, and Nathalie du Pasquier (*b.*1957) from France. Other postmodern designers, including Japan's Shiro Kuramata (1934–1991) and an American, Michael Graves, created pieces for Memphis, too.

SCRAMBLED STYLE

Memphis designers were inspired by both history and popular culture — ancient Egypt, Aztec art, comic strips, punk, and children's toys. Combining design elements from these sources with bizarre materials, they turned good taste upside down. The use of colorful plastic laminates, such as Formica, was typical of Memphis's jumbled "high" and "low" style. Before Memphis, laminates were used mainly in cafés and coffee bars.

ELVIS RULES

The name *Memphis* was typical of the group's eclectic approach. Memphis was one of the capital cities of ancient Egypt long before Memphis, Tennessee, became famous as the U.S. city where blues music was born and Elvis Presley built his Graceland home.

THE NEW SIMPLICITY

Other new design styles of the period offered simpler, more sculptural pieces made from industrial materials, such as iron, steel, sheet glass, and rubber.

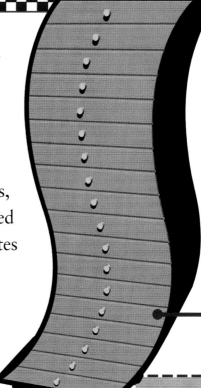

The elegant proportions and innovative form of this wavy chest of drawers made Japanese designer Shiro Kuramata famous. (Furniture in Irregular Forms, 1970) In the 1980s, Kuramata created pieces for the Memphis group, including a concrete table with embedded colored glass.

13

STREET STYLE

In 1964, British businessman and designer Terence Conran (b.1931) opened his first Habitat shop on Fulham Road in London. Habitat sold everything from furniture to curtain fabrics to cutlery and was an instant success. In the 1980s, Conran established the Conran Foundation, which funded the London Design Museum that opened in 1989.

Gae Aulenti (b.1927) is one of the few female architect-designers to achieve international fame. Aulenti gave her Table With Wheels (1980) a high-tech look by mounting its top on industrial metal and rubber casters.

The furniture and lighting in this 1980s apartment has a typically postmodern variety of color and form. (Chicago furniture designed by Cockrell)

Terence Conran in one of his apartments in 1981

GRAPHICS

As postmodernism and punk sent shock waves through the design world, radical graphic designers began to experiment with typography and page layout in magazines and books and on posters.

Wolfgang Weingart layered type and images on this poster for a 1982 exhibition of work by modernist designer Herbert Bayer.

14

LEADER OF THE PACK

German-born Wolfgang Weingart (*b.*1941) was, perhaps, the most influential graphic designer of the period. Weingart, who taught at a leading Swiss design school, challenged nearly every type convention of the day. He changed the weight of type in the middle of a word, opened up letter and word spacing, and put together collages of type and images. Weingart's students, one of whom was American graphic designer April Greiman (*b.*1948) spread his ideas internationally.

This poster advertising Benetton's "United Colors" exploited the shock value of social taboos.

The first time a heart symbol replaced the word "love" was in this famous logo, created in 1977 by American Milton Glaser (b.1929).

Thanks to low-cost photo-typesetting, visual symbols could be built into a type-face, such as this one by British designer Richard Ward. (1977)

ABCDEFGHIJKLMNOPQRSTUVWXYZ

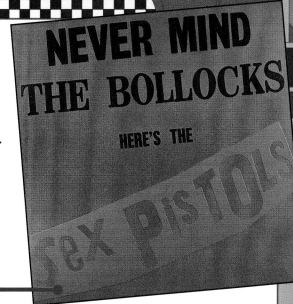

Jamie Reid was art director for the Sex Pistols when the group formed in 1975. His use of clashing colors and cut-out, blackmail-style letters captured the chaos of punk music.

UNITED COLORS OF BENETTON.

ANARCHY IN THE UNITED KINGDOM

In Britain, punk anarchy found expression in the ripped-and-pasted designs of Jamie Reid (*b.*1940). Another original British designer of the period was Neville Brody (*b.*1957), art director for *The Face* magazine from 1981 to 1986. Brody's unique page layouts and specially created logos and typefaces were mimicked throughout the world.

15

MAKING 3-D PICTURES WITH LASERS

The hologram was one of the new technologies that became available to graphic designers in the 1970s. This three-dimensional image on a two-dimensional surface was dreamed up in 1947 but did not become possible until the first working laser was developed in 1960. A hologram is made by using mirrors to split laser light into a reference beam and one or more object beams. The reference beam is directed straight at a special photographic plate; the object beams bounce off an object toward the plate. Interference between the reference and object beams makes the patterns of the hologram on the plate.

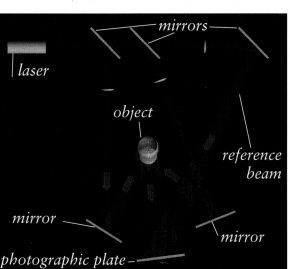

A hologram was used on the cover of National Geographic *magazine in 1985.*

ARCHITECTURE

The work of postmodern architects ranged from elegant to surreal. If any one aim united them, it was expressed by American Philip Johnson (*b.*1906) when he said "have fun, always try to get fun in." Although he had worked with Mies van der Rohe on the severely modernist Seagram Building, Johnson experimented with different architectural styles and took a new direction by the early 1980s.

Because of its shape, this New York skyscraper, designed by Philip Johnson in 1986, quickly earned the nickname "Lipstick Building." It is made of red granite, glass, and aluminum.

THE FATHER OF POSTMODERNISM

Philip Johnson is also known to have said, "we were getting bored of the box." His 646-foot (197-meter) pink granite AT&T building in New York (1978–1984) certainly broke that mold. Critics have compared it with a grandfather clock, a gravestone, and the front end of a Rolls Royce. It was the first major postmodern building. Other leading American postmodern architects were Robert Venturi, Charles Moore (*b.*1925), and Michael Graves (who designed the "singing bird" kettle for Alessi).

THE POSTMODERN WORLD

Postmodernism rapidly became an international movement. One of the leading architects in Europe was Austrian Hans Hollein (*b*.1934). Like most architects throughout the 20th century, Hollein was equally involved with both the interior and exterior design of buildings. His most famous design was the interior of the Austrian Travel Bureau in Vienna (1976–1978). Using a travel theme, Hollein's imagination ran riot. The design included a gold-roofed Indian pavilion, flying birds hanging from the ceiling, gilded palm trees, a broken classical column, and the railings of an ocean liner (complete with life buoy)!

The golden sculpture that crowns Philippe Starck's surreal design of Super Dry Hall (1989), the head-quarters of the Asahi Beer Company in Tokyo, is 140 feet (43 m) long. Shipbuilders made it using submarine construction techniques. The building is covered with black granite.

The curve of this stunning postmodern skyscraper at 333 West Wacker Drive in Chicago echoes the bend of the riverbank on which it was built. (designed by Kohn Petersen Fox Associates, 1981–1983)

The columns and arches of Charles Moore's Piazza d'Italia in New Orleans (1975–1979) pay tribute to the architectural styles of ancient Greece and Rome. Moore gave the Piazza a postmodern twist by decorating it with stainless steel, vibrant colors, and neon lights!

FUTURE VISION

Throughout the 20th century, people tried to predict how technology would shape future lifestyles. The oppressive landscape of Ridley Scott's 1982 cult film, *Blade Runner*, dominated these futuristic visions during the 1980s.

The futuristic city created for Blade Runner *is nightmarishly overcrowded and chaotic.*

INSIDE-OUT BUILDINGS

"High-tech" was another unusual architectural style developed during the 1970s. Its focus on engineering and construction was more technologically orientated than postmodernism, but the results were just as playful — buildings were literally turned inside out!

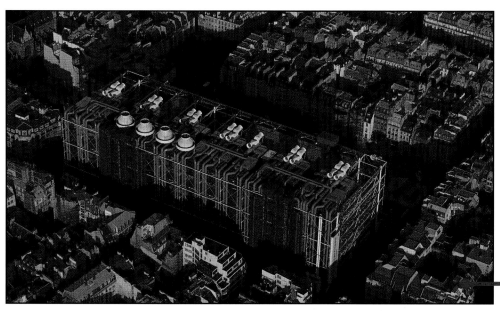

The Pompidou Center in Paris (1971–1977) houses a library, a museum, a research center, and galleries. According to its architects, Rogers and Piano, the building's colorful, inside-out design makes it look like "a giant erector set."

ARTS CENTER GOES HIGH-TECH

In the early 1970s, British architect Richard Rogers (*b*.1933) and Italian Renzo Piano (*b*.1927) created the world's most famous high-tech building, an arts complex in Paris called the Pompidou Center. This remarkable building has its structural skeleton and all of its mechanical services on the outside! Huge, color-coded pipes carry heating and air conditioning services in blue, electrical systems in yellow, and water in green. Elevator shafts are red. An external skeleton means the interior is completely free of structural supports. The huge, open-plan floors are divided only by movable partitions.

Rogers again freed internal space in his polished concrete and steel Lloyds building (London, 1978–1986) by positioning elevators and staircases on the outside.

Eight massive, external masts carry the weight of Hong Kong's spectacularly high-tech Hong Kong and Shanghai Bank, designed by Norman Foster (1979–1985). The masts are clusters of aluminum-coated steel tubes.

HIGH-TECH GOES HIGH-RISE

British architect Norman Foster (*b.*1935) designed another innovative high-tech building, the Hong Kong and Shanghai Bank. This structure's main floors are suspended from external, tubular-steel masts that rise the full height of the building — 587 feet (179 m). The masts are connected by suspension trusses that look and work like coat hangers.

MAKING STEEL STRUCTURES SAFE

The heat of a fire causes steel to lose its strength. To protect steel parts of a building against fire, the steel can be: (**1**) encased in concrete, (**2**) wrapped in heat-resistant panels, or (**3**) sprayed with a fireproof substance. (**4**) The tubular-steel support beams at the Pompidou Center were filled with water to absorb heat energy and keep the steel cool.

1   2   3   4

INFORMATION TECHNOLOGY

The first electronic computers, built during the final years of World War II (1939–1945), were huge, room-sized machines. By the early 1970s, however, technological advancements had brought on a new age of miniaturized electronic components and the development of the microprocessor.

Computers dramatically changed life in the office.

MINIATURE CONTROL CENTER

A microprocessor is a microchip, or a group of microchips, that controls all of a computer's operations. It is the central processing unit (CPU) or "brain" of a computer. In 1971, the Intel Corporation launched Intel 4004, the first microprocessor sold in the United States.

A microchip is a tiny sliver of silicon containing the thousands of components that make an electronic circuit.

Apple's first PC, Apple 1, debuted in 1976. In 1984, Apple introduced the Macintosh, or Mac, which was styled by the German group frogdesign (f.1969).

Macintosh Plus

CHIPS WITH EVERYTHING

Engineers used microchips to make computers smaller and less expensive, paving the way for the introduction of the PC (personal computer) in the mid 1970s and early 1980s. Soon microchips were controlling everything from traffic lights to washing machines.

LASER TECHNOLOGY

Although a number of scientists worked to develop the laser, American engineer Theodore Maiman (*b*.1927) was the first to build a working laser, in 1960. Today, computer printers, bar code scanners, and compact discs (CDs) all use laser technology. Laser beams carry telephone, computer, and TV signals along fiber-optic cables. Fiber-optic technology was developed in the 1960s and early 1970s. The first optical fiber trunk cable for telecommunications was installed in 1976. One hundred fibers make up a single cable only 0.4 inch (10 millimeters) thick. This thin cable can carry as much information as twenty thousand of the old-fashioned copper wires.

Lasers are used not only for measuring, cutting, and drilling, but also for satellite tracking, eye surgery, and holography.

OPTICAL FIBER TECHNOLOGY

Optical fibers rely on light waves refracting, or changing direction, when they pass from one medium to another. A single optical fiber is a flexible, hairlike strand of highly refractive glass or plastic covered with a less refractive material. The covering acts like a mirror, continually bouncing light back into the fiber's core. At one end of the fiber, a laser device transforms electrical digital pulses into light pulses. The light pulses are reversed by a photodetector at the other end.

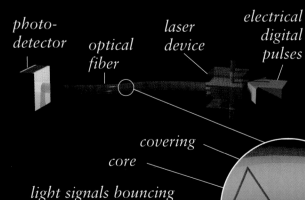

photo-detector *optical fiber* *laser device* *electrical digital pulses*

covering
core
light signals bouncing off covering

CHIPS AND LCDs

Microchips revolutionized the production of electronic devices. Manufacturers used them in an incredible variety of products. Besides computers, microchips transformed calculators, camcorders, televisions, telephones, washing machines, microwave ovens — even cars.

In the 1980s, watches by the Swiss company Swatch were must-have fashion accessories. These colorful watches were powered by vibrations from a quartz crystal.

VIDEO WAR GAMES

The first home videocassette recorders (VCRs) went on sale in the early 1970s. In 1976, two Japanese companies launched new systems, starting a battle for market leadership. JVC's video home system (VHS) won over Sony's Betamax.

Video cameras record sounds and images on magnetic videotape.

SMALL IS BEAUTIFUL

The miniaturization of electronic components meant that the housing of a product was no longer dictated by its inner workings. Now industrial designers were free to explore product styling, and a new era dawned in which machines were fashionable as well as functional.

JAPANESE TREND SETTERS

The Japanese company Sony led the fashionable electronics movement when it created one of the first electronic fashion accessories, the "Walkman" personal stereo. Sony chairman and founder, Akio Morita, has been given credit for the idea.

Launched in 1979, the Sony Walkman was the first personal cassette player. Originally styled by the Sony Design Center, its look is still evolving today — to keep pace with changing fashions.

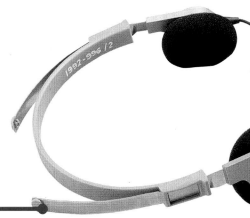

In 1987, Italian architect-designer Mario Bellini (b.1935) styled the ETP55 compact, portable electronic typewriter for the Olivetti company.

This Braun pocket calculator, designed by German Dieter Rams (b.1932) in the late 1970s, had a liquid crystal display.

MYSTERIOUS CRYSTALS

Another technological breakthrough — liquid crystals — also transformed electronic devices of the period. Although scientists discovered liquid crystals in the 1850s, the first practical ones were not developed until the early 1970s. Liquid crystal displays (LCDs), which are wafer thin and need very little power, were quickly added to watches and pocket calculators.

liquid crystal display

LIQUID-CRYSTAL TECHNOLOGY

A black-and-white LCD is made up of groups of electrode segments. Inside each segment, liquid crystals are sandwiched between pairs of transparent electrodes and polarizing filters. The filters are positioned at right angles to each other. When there is no electric charge, the crystals twist light so it passes through both filters and reflects off the mirror, displaying no image. An electric charge changes the crystals so they stop light from passing through the bottom filter, displaying a black image. Applying charges to groups of segments forms numbers and characters.

light
light
polarizing sheets
transparent electrodes
liquid crystals
transparent electrodes
polarizing sheets
mirrors

charge applied — no light reflected
no charge — light reflected

ALTERNATIVE POWER

In 1973, the Organization of Petroleum Exporting Countries (OPEC) raised oil prices by more than two hundred percent and began to restrict oil production. Resulting fuel shortages caused an economic crisis in industrial nations all over the world.

In Brazil, the oil crisis revived research into making fuel for cars out of alcohol distilled from fermented sugarcane juice.

24

GREEN MOVEMENTS

The oil crisis fed a growing concern about Earth's natural resources and prompted increased support for environmental movements and for research into alternative sources of power. Canadian opponents of nuclear testing formed Greenpeace in 1971, and the world's first Green political party was founded in West Germany in 1979.

Electromagnets propel maglev trains, which first began running during the 1970s. The technology was developed in Britain, Japan, and Germany.

MLU
002

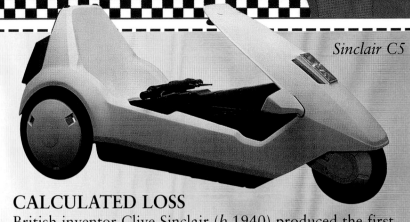

CALCULATED LOSS

British inventor Clive Sinclair (*b*.1940) produced the first pocket-sized calculator in 1972. Later, he made personal computers. His battery-powered car, Sinclair C5 (1985), was less successful — production stopped within months.

In 1979, a team of Americans completed the first pedal-powered flight across the English Channel in this plane, the Gossamer Albatross. *The team's next plane,* Solar Challenger, *used pedal and solar power.*

Australia hosted the world's first trans-continental race for solar-powered cars in 1987.

GREEN POWER

Fossil fuels, such as oil, are nonrenewable resources that pollute the environment. Research in the 1970s and 1980s looked at clean, renewable power sources, such as solar, wind, wave, and tidal energy.

GREEN TRANSPORTATION

Engineers worked on everything from battery-powered electric cars to solar cars and airplanes trying to develop alternative forms of transportation. In rail transportation, one of the most exciting developments since the steam train was "magnetic levitation," or maglev. Friction between a train's wheels and the tracks wastes energy. Maglev trains reduce friction by floating above the track.

25

THE SCIENCE OF LEVITATION

The maglev system is based on the scientific fact that like poles (positive or negative) of a magnet repel, and opposite poles attract. Maglev uses powerful levitation and driving electromagnets. One set of each type is in the track; another set is in the train. In most maglev trains, levitation comes from like magnetic poles repelling each other, forcing the train and the track apart. Drive comes from the pull and push of alternating positive and negative poles. Positive poles in the track pull (attract) the train forward. Then, as the train passes over the track's negative poles, it is pushed (repelled) onward.

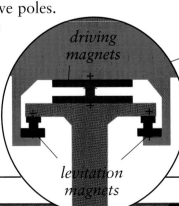

driving magnets

levitation magnets

HIGH-TECH PEOPLE MOVERS

Although the basic shape of most airliners has barely changed since the 1950s, a revolution has taken place in their construction. Innovations of the 1970s and 1980s include the use of high-tech materials and computerized control systems.

The first flight of an A320 was on February 22, 1987.

Strong, lightweight, high-tech materials reduce weight, which saves fuel. These materials were used in the A320 for everything from wings and tail fins to brakes and engine mountings.

26

THE FLYING COMPUTER

The A320, built by Airbus Industries, was the first passenger plane to have fly-by-wire technology. Before the A320, pilots controlled a plane's movements manually, with a large, central joystick. A fly-by-wire plane has a small side stick connected to a flight computer. The computer reads the movements of the side stick and controls the plane electronically. Nearly everything on the A320 was computerized. Computers told the crew where they were, what condition they were in, and even where they were likely to end up!

Airbus Industries is an international group of companies. Parts of the A320 were made by each company in its own country. This special plane, the Guppy, moved the parts to Toulouse, France, for final assembly.

ROBOTS — FROM TOY TO COWORKER

Although mechanical automatons were being made as long ago as ancient Greek times, they were not called "robots" until 1920, when Czech playwright Karel Capek coined the word from the Czech *robota*, meaning "forced labor." The first robot to use a tool (for painting) was put to work in Norway in 1966. Since then, computer-controlled robots have been developed to do everything from brain surgery to playing the piano and shearing sheep!

Since the 1960s, industrial robots have been used for tasks such as welding and assembling electronic parts.

HIGH-SPEED LAND TRAVEL

Back in the 1970s and 1980s, the fastest way to travel on land was by electric train. Electricity from overhead cables powered traction motors to drive the train's wheels. Electric trains doubled the speed record of 125 miles (201 km) per hour set by the British steam locomotive *Mallard* in 1938. In 1988, Germany's ICE electric train reached 252 miles (406 km) per hour, and the French TGV (*Train à Grande Vitesse*) managed an astonishing 320 miles (515 km) per hour in 1990.

The French high-speed electric train, the TGV, first ran in 1981. Normal speed was about 130 miles (210 km) per hour.

Britain's high-speed electric train, the 125, started running in 1976. British industrial designer Kenneth Grange (b.1929) styled the exterior.

27

SPACE TRAVEL

Space exploration, boosted by technological developments, took giant leaps forward during the 1970s and 1980s. Both the United States and the USSR launched unmanned spacecraft and sent probes to Venus and Mars. The U.S. also sent probes to Mercury and to Jupiter and the other gas giants.

28

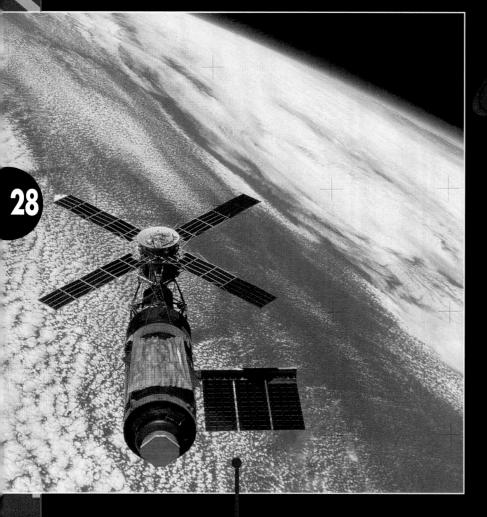

The American space station Skylab, *launched in 1973, completed three missions. In 1978, while attempting to shift its orbit,* Skylab *fell back to Earth and was destroyed in the atmosphere.*

The U.S. launched two Voyager probes in 1979. Both visited Jupiter and Saturn, then set course for Uranus, Neptune, and the edge of the solar system.

REMOTE CONTROL

In space, the probes were powered mainly by solar panels, but gas jets were used to make course corrections. Commands were sent by radio from Earth to onboard computers.

SPACE WORKERS

Both the United States and the USSR built robots and put them to work in space. In 1976, two robot landers from the U.S. Viking probes explored the surface of Mars. In 1981, two Soviet Venera landers scooped up soil samples from Venus. At the same time, Americans and Soviets sent human workers into space, too. In 1971, the USSR put the first of its several manned Salyut space stations into Earth's orbit. In 1973, the U.S. launched *Skylab*, its only manned space station. The Soviet's *Mir* space station followed in 1986.

THE PRICE OF SUCCESS

Using most of NASA's budget in the 1970s to develop space shuttle technology, the U.S. fell behind the USSR in space station technology. By the time the first Shuttle, *Columbia*, was launched, in 1981, the program had cost nearly $10 billion! Although the cost of development was high — and the Shuttle needed ten times as much fuel as a jumbo jet — it was worth it. *Columbia* took off like a rocket, cruised like a spacecraft, and landed like a glider. Most importantly, however, it was the world's first reusable spacecraft.

When two Viking landers touched down on Mars in 1976, they photographed the planet's surface, reported on its weather, and tested soil samples for signs of life.

THREE-STAGE JOURNEY FOR A REVOLUTIONARY SPACE MACHINE

The main parts of the Space Shuttle are the orbiter (which carries the crew and the payload), solid fuel rocket boosters (SRBs), and an external, liquid fuel tank (ET). At liftoff, the orbiter and the SRBs are attached to the ET. (**1**) The SRBs provide most of the thrust for liftoff, but, soon after, they are released and parachute into the ocean, where they are collected and reused. (**2**) Reaching orbit, the ET is jettisoned and destroyed by heat as it falls through Earth's atmosphere, and the orbiter goes on to conduct scientific experiments and to launch satellites and other equipment. (**3**) The orbiter is protected by about 23,000 ceramic-coated, heat-resistant tiles as it reenters Earth's atmosphere and glides down to land on a runway.

1

2

3

· T I M E L I N E ·

	DESIGN	WORLD EVENTS	TECHNOLOGY	FAMOUS PEOPLE	ART & MEDIA
1970	•*Shiro Kuramata:* irregular furniture	•*U.S. troops sent into Cambodia*		•*The Beatles split* •*Janis Joplin and Jimi Hendrix die*	•*Germaine Greer:* The Female Eunuch
1971	•*Vivienne Westwood opens her first shop*	•*Uganda: Amin in power* •*Greenpeace founded*	•*First microprocessor* •*USSR: Salyut 1 space station*	•*Ali loses world heavyweight title to Frazier*	•*David Bowie:* Starman •*Kubrick: A Clockwork Orange*
1972	•*Richard Sapper: Tizio table lamp*	•*Direct rule in Ulster* •*U.S. troops leave Vietnam*	•*First video game* •*First pocket calculator*	•*Mark Spitz wins seven gold medals at Munich Olympics*	•*Francis Ford Coppola:* The Godfather
1973	•*Issey Miyake's first fashion show in Paris*	•*Yom Kippur War* •*OPEC raises oil prices*	•*U.S.: Skylab space station*	•*Salvador Allende assassinated*	•*Thomas Pynchon:* Gravity's Rainbow
1974	•*Des-in studio: Tire sofa*	•*Turkey invades Cyprus and occupies one-third*	•*Bar code scanners first used in supermarkets*	•*U.S. president Nixon resigns over Watergate*	•*Fellini: Amarcord* •*ABBA: Waterloo*
1975	•*Jamie Reid becomes art director for Sex Pistols*	•*Cambodia overrun by Pol Pot's Khmer Rouge*	•*First small home computer, the Altair*	•*Bill Gates and Paul Allen found Microsoft*	•*Steven Spielberg:* Jaws •*Queen:* Bohemian Rhapsody
1976	•*Kenneth Grange styles high-speed 125 train*	•*South Africa: Soweto uprising*	•*First fiber-optic trunk cable for telecommunications*	•*Steven Jobs and Steven Wozniak found Apple*	•*Christo:* Running Fence *environmental sculpture*
1977	•*Rogers and Piano: Pompidou Centre*	•*UN bans arms sales to South Africa*	•*First human-powered flight, in Gossamer Condor*	•*Steve Biko dies in South African police custody*	•*Sex Pistols:* God Save the Queen *banned by BBC*
1978	•*Philip Johnson begins AT&T skyscraper*	•*Egypt and Israel sign Camp David peace treaty*		•*First test-tube baby, Louise Brown, born*	•*John Travolta:* Saturday Night Fever
1979	•*Charles Moore: Piazza d'Italia*	•*Iran: Khomeini in power* •*USSR invades Afghanistan*	•*Sony Walkman invented*	•*Thatcher becomes Britain's first woman prime minister*	•*Woody Allen:* Manhattan
1980	•*Gae Aulenti: Table With Wheels*	•*Start of Iran-Iraq War* •*Poland: Solidarity*	•*First portable computer, the Sharp PC 1211*	•*John Lennon shot*	•*Anthony Burgess:* Earthly Powers
1981	•*Memphis design group founded*	•*Egypt: President Sadat assassinated*	•*U.S.: First Space Shuttle, Columbia, launched*	•*Prince Charles and Lady Diana marry*	•*Rushdie:* Midnight's Children •*The Face launched*
1982	•*Tadao Ando: Kidosaki House in Tokyo*	•*Falklands War: Britain defeats Argentina*	•*First artificial heart transplant*	•*Princess Grace of Monaco dies*	•*Ridley Scott:* Blade Runner •*Spielberg:* E.T.
1983	•*E. Sottsass: Bay lamp* •*Swatch watch*	•*U.S. and Caribbean troops invade Grenada*	•*CDs first go on sale* •*AIDS virus isolated*	•*Lech Walesa awarded Nobel Peace Prize*	•*Merce Cunningham:* Quartets *dance pieces*
1984	•*James Dyson: G Force bagless vacuum cleaner*	•*New Zealand declared a nuclear-free zone*	•*Apple Macintosh, styled by frogdesign*	•*Bob Geldof sets up Band Aid pop charity*	•*Madonna:* Like a Virgin •*Philip Glass:* Akhnaten
1985	•*Michael Graves: kettle with singing bird*	•*USSR: Gorbachev named Communist Party secretary*	•*Battery-powered Sinclair C5* •*Ozone layer hole confirmed*	•*Orson Welles dies*	•*Lucien Freud:* Self-Portrait •*Arvo Pärt:* Stabat Mater
1986	•*Richard Rogers: Lloyds Building*	•*USSR: Chernobyl nuclear disaster*	•*Space Shuttle Challenger explodes*	•*Cory Aquino wins Philippines elections*	•*Jeff Koons:* Rabbit
1987	•*Tom Dixon: S chair*	•*Black Monday stock market crash*	•*First flight of fly-by-wire A320 plane*	•*Terry Waite taken hostage in Beirut*	•*Toni Morrison:* Beloved
1988	•*Philippe Starck: Royalton Hotel in New York*	•*End of Iran-Iraq War* •*Lockerbie air disaster*	•*Stephen Hawking: A Brief History of Time*	•*Pakistan: Bhutto named prime minister*	•*Iris Murdoch:* The Book and the Brotherhood
1989	•*Design Museum opens in London*	•*China: Tiananmen Square massacre*	•*Nintendo launches Game Boy*	•*Khomeini dies*	•*Helen Chadwick:* Enfleshings

GLOSSARY

automatons: machines or mechanical devices that are almost self-operating and often mimic the movements of living beings; robots.

eclectic: made up of a variety of styles, often drawn from diverse sources, that are considered "the best" of their type or class.

haute couture: high fashion; trend-setting fashions by well-known and exclusive designers.

kitsch: of poor taste or low quality, often crude or gaudy; having popular appeal to a mass market.

laminates: (n) materials made by compressing and bonding together many thin layers of one or more materials, especially wood or plastic.

laser: a mechanical device that directs light through a crystal to create a very narrow beam of intensified light radiation that is so strong it can cut or drill through materials as hard as diamonds.

lurid: having a shockingly vivid appearance that is sometimes unnatural, ghastly, or revolting.

microprocessor: the central processing unit (CPU) or brain of a computer, which contains one or more microchips and controls all of the computer's operating functions.

payload: objects or freight, such as passengers or instruments, carried in an aircraft or a spacecraft that are not necessary to the operation of the craft but are necessary to the purpose of the flight.

prototype: an original model of a product, which is subsequently copied to mass-produce the product.

surreal: having the feel or appearance of thought that is irrational, subconscious, or dreamlike.

titanium: a strong, lightweight, silver-gray metallic element that is often combined with other metals to make corrosion-resistant alloys and coatings.

MORE BOOKS TO READ

6 Chapters in Design. Saul Bass, Ivan Chermayeff, Milton Glaser, Paul Rand, Ikko Tanaka, and Philip B. Meggs (Chronicle Books)

The 70s: Punks, Glam Rockers, & New Romantics. 20th Century Fashion (series). Sarah Gilmour (Gareth Stevens)

The Computer Age. Modern Media (series). (Barrons)

Discovering the Universe. An Inside Look (series). Stuart G. Clark (Gareth Stevens)

High-Speed Trains. The World's Railroads (series). Christopher Chant (Chelsea House)

Lasers. 20th Century Inventions (series). Nina Morgan (Raintree/Steck-Vaughn)

Memphis: Research, Experiences, Failures and Successes of New Design. Barbara Radice (Thames and Hudson)

Mountain Biking. First Book (series). Larry Dane Brimner and Abramowski Dwain (Franklin Watts)

Philip Johnson: The Architect in His Own Words. Philip Johnson, Hilary Lewis, and John T. O'Connor (Rizzoli Publications)

Starck. Conway Lloyd Morgan (Universe)

WEB SITES

The Internet Webseum of Holography. *www.enter.net/~holostudio*

Make a MagLev Train. *k12.magnet.fsu.edu/ student/inter/maglev.html*

Paul Hughes Fine Art: Shiro Kuramata. *www.paulhughes.co.uk/conthome/kuramata/ shiro.html*

retromodern.com. *www.20thcenturydesign.com*

Due to the dynamic nature of the Internet, some web sites stay current longer than others. To find additional web sites, use a reliable search engine with one or more of the following keywords: *A320, disco fashion, holograms, Philip Johnson, lasers, liquid crystal, maglev, Memphis design, the 1970s, the 1980s, postmodernism, Jamie Reid,* and *space shuttle.*

INDEX